ALTERED CONSCIENCE

ALTERED CONSCIENCE

REGINALD L. RUSSELL

The evolution of Reginald Russell derived from his innermost thoughts, expressed in original poems—all in his own words

Luke 23
LUKE 23 PUBLISHING
COMPANY LLC

Altered Conscience
Copyright © 2016 by Reginald L. Russell. All rights reserved.

No part of this publication may be reproduced, stored in a retrieval system or transmitted in any way by any means: electronic, mechanical, photocopy, recording or otherwise without the prior permission of the author except as provided by USA copyright law.

This book is designed to provide accurate and authoritative information with regard to the subject matter covered. This information is given with the understanding that neither the author nor Luke 23 Publishing Company, LLC is engaged in rendering legal, professional advice.

Since the details of your situation are fact dependent, you should additionally seek the services of a competent professional.

The opinions expressed by the author are not necessarily those of Luke 23 Publishing Company, LLC.

Published by Luke 23 Publishing Company, LLC.

The company is committed to excellence in the publishing industry. The company reflects the philosophy established by the gospel of Christ, based on Luke 23:46 *"Father, unto thy hands I commend my spirit"*.

Book design copyright © by Luke 23 Publishing Company, LLC. All rights reserved.

Cover design by: Luke 23 Publishing Company, LLC.

Interior design: Luke 23 Publishing Company, LLC.

Published in the United States of America

ISBN: 978-0-9990486-0-3

1. Poetry / Subjects & Themes / Inspirational & Religious
2. Poetry / American / African American

15.11.10

ACKNOWLEDGMENTS

I want to take the time to thank those who are and were of great influence in my life. I want to pay homage to my grandparents, Willie Mack and Georgia Mae Woods. Without their continued love and support, prayers, and righteous living, I would definitely have been bound to the surroundings of my youth. I want to thank my father and mother, Gregory Lynn and Willie Mae Russell, for raising up a child in the way that he should go. Thank you for believing in me when no one else would; thank you for allowing me to visualize my greatness! Last but not least, I want to thank my brothers, Darwin and Trenton Russell. These two are my inspiration in so many ways. Thank you for always being genuinely big brothers to me. This piece of me is dedicated to you all; thank you from the very depths of my soul!

CONTENTS

Foreword	9
Introduction: My Life	11
I Understand	12
The Escape	13
Blind Divinity	14
Brief Realization	15
True Love	16
Cognizant	17
Purgative	18
Reasons	19
Empty Interaction	21
Dysfunctional Function	22
Stronghold of Sin	23
Brief Illumination	24
Blind Vision	25
Ready	27
Controversy	28
Provided	30
Rejuvenated Soul	32
Anew	34
?Questions?	35
Haystack	37
Reggie's Prayer	39
Reggie's Prayer 2	40

Tell Me: Part 1	43
Tell Me: Part 2	45
Course	48
Dreams	50
Trouble	53
Rain Down	55
Dreams and Wonders	57
Doth Follow	59
Do You Know Me?	60
Caught	61
Never Thought	65
My Dream	66
The Perfect Change!	68
Black World	70
If Never	72
One Face	73
Strive	75
Blind Eyes	77
Oh, How Real	78
My Day	80
Momma, Why My Heart?	81
Realism	82
How I Lost My Will	83
All Stars Must Fall #94 Russell	85
Thank You	87

FOREWORD

Altered Conscience, a book of poems, written from personal experiences of the writer.

Feelings and parodies intended to depict the many stages of a young mind growing up in a world that appears to be a jungle of primitive, inexplicable relationships with family, friends, and foes!

The ever-changing emotions of love, anger, hate, disappointments, and confusion, as viewed by an adolescent evolving into a man.

These life experiences that appear to be altered in the mind's eye will keep the reader captivated until the last one is read.

—Patricia Robertson

Altered Conscience

INTRODUCTION: MY LIFE

My life has taken me many places.
It has taken me to the land of hope,
Hoping that life would be full of happiness.
My life has taken me to the island of love,
In which my heart has colonized,
Unable to let just anyone enter.

My life has sailed me to mercy,
Where my actions were accepted.
My life has flown in the clouds of care,
Where my feelings were massaged.
And from that act,
I was allowed to feel for others.

My life,
My life has taken me many places.
I have been through the slums of Hell on Earth.
I have visualized Heaven,
With its streets of paved gold.
I have talked with God Almighty.
I made reservations.
This is the place that I will take my life.

Reginald L. Russell

I UNDERSTAND

When my pops was clean,
I saw glimpses of his true heart.
Just like the night and day,
I could tell my daddy's lives apart.
His struggle between right and wrong,
And his passion to alter his conscience
From the conflict involved in living life!

I can't excuse being weak
I can't excuse being strong.
Life shifts those curses on us all!

Believe me,
Your life won't always be filled with strength
If so, your life exceeded even that
Which Jesus lived.

Allow your heart and mind
To orchestrate a true understanding
Of life's inconsistencies.
Our true goal in life
Is to embody our souls to the truth
A journey that ships us home
To live again In Yahweh's precious arms.

Altered Conscience

THE ESCAPE

I calculate my faults
While realizing my troubles!
Born to be disadvantaged,
I learn to live with my struggles.

I believe my life has an identity
Unfamiliar to the world.
Can I conquer my crisis,
And escape to serenity?
I underestimate the strength
That's been given to me.

How do I convince myself to claim my right
Through the cost that has been paid?
Oh, God, block my heart
From the devil's evil ways!

My soul aches while realizing
How strong my flesh is
Within its weakness!
I concentrate on consecration,
Praying that my God would uplift me.

Reginald L. Russell

I stretch forth my fist,
Clenched with dirt.
Father, wipe my hand
With your heavenly cloak!
Though I'm dirty,
I desire still to be clean.
Acknowledge my heart, father,
And provide what my life needs!

Altered Conscience

BLIND DIVINITY

I kicked my cool to the curb!
No longer desiring to be hip with the verb!
Put on a new hat,
I looked back at myself once again,
As I started my new journey.
Using life as a tool
To claim my birthright.
Offending God
So that he'd arrest me!

How much longer will it take?
I have abused my privilege
Of being a Christian.
Touch me, Lord
Seal my mouth, carry me,
And show me how to walk!
Blend my soul with divinity
And create something like you within me!

Evidence is what I need
To sustain my faith.
Though I'm walking without sight,
I still need to feel
And taste what is of you.

Reginald L. Russell

BRIEF REALIZATION

I talked to my brother last night. He called,
After I'd just got through smoking on a blunt,
Which is something I told myself
I didn't ever want to do again!
He spoke to me
About some issues in my family.
He told me that my only grand-father
Had been diagnosed with cancer,
The same kind of cancer
That my grandmother,
His wife, died from.

And he told me that my cousin, Floyd,
Had been diagnosed with throat cancer
And that the doctors had given them both
Six months to a year to live
With the disease!

Altered Conscience

In my mind,
All my problems all of a sudden
Weren't as extreme as they'd seemed
Before I had spoken to my brother.
I began to converse more with my brother
And told him that I felt so selfish. I felt bad,
Because of the amount of energy
I spent on myself worrying
About my small problems.
It seemed to me that,
Through my acknowledging this truth,
My problems were no longer as important.

Reginald L. Russell

TRUE LOVE

Lost in love, or so I think.
I'm afraid I'll miss something
At my next eyes' blink.
How do I fight to figure my true love?
My heart has risen for only a few,
Tackled with a reality of a playboy's mentality;
I search for true love without a clue!

Since the genesis
Of my heart's intimate mechanism,
I've left bits and pieces
At the doorstep of many a fair maiden.
Clever, many may think.
But to my heart,
Ridiculous is the plea!

Very descriptive in my desire for an ideal mate,
But I am blinded by my acts of fornication.
I pull all traits desired from women of my familiarity,
Never able to indulge in the totality of the feminine fruit!

Altered Conscience

COGNIZANT

Lord, however was I able
To turn from your light?
To embrace wickedness
And hide from your love?
You've kept me
When it seemed that no one cared.
You have allowed me to embrace
A dream of deliverance,
In the midst of my sinful ways.
You rebuked my disobedience through love!
I shout unto he who listens
The goodness of the Lord,
My God.

Father, as I roamed the kingdom of Satan,
Numbed from your spirit
By the cloud of my iniquity,
I held on to the remembrance
Of your comfort.
I held on to the victory of Christ!
You allowed me to experience
Life's trauma in my youth.
I now understand that
Purpose is greater in you
Than in Satan's dungeon
Of misconception.

Reginald L. Russell

I hold now, father,
That you are my rock
And my salvation,
And nowhere can I be received
Lest be through you.
I understand that
No longer can I run
And hide from your words of prophecy.
I acknowledge that my purpose
Be only through you.

I shall now submit
My ear and my voice
To the echo of Calvary's purpose.
I now render unto you fully my life
As a complete and total sacrifice.

Lord, deliver me always
From evil temptation.
Allow my feet to be quick
In response to your will.
Hold me high

So that my enemies might believe
In your goodness!
In the name of Christ, I pray.
Amen!

Altered Conscience

PURGATIVE

Dreams locked behind the door of despair,
Clawing to claim my birthright
And leave life's idiocy
To the raw of foolishness.
I feel that my life has brought me
A greater purpose, than most.

How do I end the struggle
To obtain my revelation
And walk in belief?
The root of my life starts
With the knowledge
Of what's wrong and what's right.
I've pledged my heart
To remain conscious,
Allowing me liberty of action.
I follow the Master's Plan!

I invest in reality
To subtract any
Misconception or disillusionment,
Holding tight to the truth,
For it costs me nothing!

Reginald L. Russell

Bring me love separate from the pain.
Bring me hope separate from strain,
Fulfilled to fulfill my life's claim.
Penetrate me, father,
To rearrange my heart.

Altered Conscience

REASONS

Explore love. Dream expensively.
Follow life's most intimate desires.
Just hope you don't expire.
Tomorrow, my brother,
Is as fresh as a newly found treasure.

Under my heart, I bury purpose
And yield to self-gratification,
Chipping away at time designed
For edification of my father's body,
Indulged in Satan's plan for destruction.

I feel my faith has been abandoned.
A transformation has taken place,
And it has left me alone.

So I swim in my iniquities.
I've become a zombie.
I don't dream, react, or aspire the way I used to.
Not even the sweet smelling fragrance
Of the roses in the garden
Has remained the same.
So I ask myself of this thing called change.

Reginald L. Russell

Change is a peculiar thing!
You can either change, change
Or let change, change you.

I eliminate what my heart says
To react without a clue.
It's evident that the obstinacies
That surround my life will bury me,
Yet I do not care.
A field of fortune
Is what my dreams provide.
When I look up,
I see reasons engraved in the sky
For why I live.

I once hid my face from reality,
Turned my back on sincerity,
And allowed no room for love!
I think to myself repetitiously
On how I could have done this.
I hope one day to know.
It once seemed that
Dreams would fall faint
At the vision of my life.
My pathway to righteousness is clogged

Altered Conscience

By an illusion of the unattainable.
But when I look up,
I see reasons engraved in the sky
For why I live.

Spewed out of the mouth of Satan
Once he bit down on my anointed core.
Finally, I figure what he needs me for.
I thank God for his design
And love him for his truths.
He separates me from the common man
And gives me a job to do!

Reginald L. Russell

EMPTY INTERACTION

Last night I felt a kiss,
It wasn't from you,
I must admit.
She grabbed my lips just like you,
Put my hands on the curve of her waist,
And told me to squeeze!

I tried to fight it,
But you weren't there,
Right at the time I needed love
And did not care.
It was scary that she could make me feel
The same way that you do,
But you aren't here,
And she is.
What am I to do?

In the morning
I woke to a wonderful feelin'.
I felt the power of love.
I instantaneously thought of you
As the scent from last night's love makin'
Showed me the truth,
But all I can think about is you!

Altered Conscience

It's night time again.
I still feel the sensation of her body
It's crazy,
But I want some more.
She told me I was gonna feel this way.
I, for the life of me,
Can't figure why she didn't stay.

Reginald L. Russell

DYSFUNCTIONAL FUNCTION

If you've investigated my life,
I guess that gives you permission to speak!
If you can determine how my heart beats
And provide a smile,
Maybe I'll stay awhile.

I'm a dreamer, baby!
That's all I know how to be.
I first started dreaming of a new life
When I first encountered pain and strife!

My life growing up
Depended on heroin and cocaine
To dull the pain,
As I watched my father abuse
Again and again.

As I grew up,
I was destined to change,
But I chose alcohol
And marijuana to dull my pain!

Altered Conscience

Now I have a son,
And I dream about him.
I wonder if my father
Ever dreamt of me,
will he be able to break
This generational curse
Of chemical dependency?

Though I am an addict,
I will for a change.
Most would consider this strange,
The want to rearrange!
My dysfunctional function!

Reginald L. Russell

STRONGHOLD OF SIN

My life has evolved
From choices that I've made.
Blind to the reality of my soul decaying,
I live to exist in sorrow.

I push my inheritance
Back until tomorrow,
Figuring that mine own satisfaction
Needed priority
Over divinity.

Why won't someone throw me a bone
I can't die full! I've got to die empty.
I know what is required of me,
But initiative is what I lack.

Tears fall; muscles grow weak.
Strongholds are built up
As clay surrounds my feet.
I wonder how God deals
With a child like me
Evidence in my life
Proves my disobedience
Or inability to consistently
Desire what is right.

Altered Conscience

BRIEF ILLUMINATION

I hesitate to allow my light to shine,
All awhile sharp images of the sun
Illuminate my mind.

As a child,
My brain was drilled on how to be.
My mother and father wanted to ensure that
Their son's life would be structured by Christianity.

Now I roam the world-free
To make my own choice,
Most times not acknowledging God's voice.
Puzzled by a puzzle,
Providing a mound for my life's rubble.

Sometimes I shout
And speak words of good nature.
I wonder if God has stamped
His own will on my life
Without me consenting to his favor?
How can I give off anything good
If bad is in my nature?

Reginald L. Russell

BLIND VISION

I brought forth an honest commitment
Knowing when my neck was put in the noose.
That it would be twisted.
I'm gifted with everything that I do.

If the pressures of life
Can't build me to strength,
What do they build me to?
I've built my life
From what I thought would be fulfilling,
Not understanding,
That my Lord wasn't always willing?

I pray, but my prayers hit the ceiling.
I conceal weapon, but mostly I'm chillin'.
I escape often; I left the "hood"
To avoid an eternal chill from a coffin.
My life has amazed itself through conflict,
Choosing an outlet of persistent
Influence to create a balance.

I'm drowning
Tryin' to keep my head above the water.
I understand new ways of living
From the days that I've bartered.
Exchanging a new faith
From a faith that was slaughtered.

Altered Conscience

I'm walking,
Trying to reach my "Heavenly Father."
I ask for guidance,
And it seems that I'm led
But something strange happens.

When I turn my head.
My momma taught me
How to drive on one road.
While driving,
I constantly glance
In the rearview mirror,
Sometimes losing direction
As I stumble over feelings.
I conclude an illusion to enlighten my path.

Reginald L. Russell

READY

O' Hearken not your heart saints
The hour of the day
Is not yet full of dismay!
Let us all rejoice in the Lord,
For our father is coming soon.
Soon all hate and sin shall be off of our face,
And we shall all rejoice in the Lord.

Soon all time to correct will be up
And those of us who still hold
Our cup in our hands
Shall join in the march
Towards the promise land.
And we will look back
Upon the times in our lives
When it was so hard to stand
And say I made it.

Altered Conscience

CONTROVERSY

Man, oh man,
It seems to me as if things never change
How could this claim itself to be true?
I have heard this said before
That "when it rains, it pours."
And this I know to be true!
When I right the wrong
I always ever so clearly
In the back of my mind
Think on the possibility
Of the wrong re-wronging itself.

See, things in life work
In strange ways sometimes.
The only real thing that
we have to clinch on to is hope.
You see, I like "hope"
Because hope never makes any promises,
So logically he doesn't have to break any.

He's just something that offers himself
To everyone who so desires him.
Providing a set of new wheels
For the car with the longest journey.

Reginald L. Russell

That brings me to my case and point.
Why would one write about dimensions
And new worlds along with state of minds?
If this is all that we are going to experience
Here on Earth?
"This" meaning the life
That we are presently living.

Although those types of writings are good,
They aren't worth the paper
That they are written on.
Humans are always trying to venture off
And explore something different
Rather than deal with the things
That we presently are involved with
So that's why in everything I do
I make sure that I stay true first to God
And secondly to myself
And have hope that all that is left
Will fall in its place.

Altered Conscience

PROVIDED

Where on this journey of hardened Heart,
Broken mind, and tired soul
Did the struggle between right and wrong
So ever cease to exist?
The struggle between the heart,
Mind, body, and soul
On this desolate, barren tomb we call earth
Has instituted a keen sense of nothingness
In the meaning of our lives.

Day in and day out
We seem to lose focus
On the source of that
Toward which we should direct
All of our energy and attention.

The element of this ol' earth,
The spiritual "we"
Have created images of extreme distraction
To ease the realization of our disobedience,
And in doing this we wonder
Why our lives are the way they are.

Reginald L. Russell

True indeed,
It hurts not to have access
To the finer things of life.
But in proclamation of my situation,
I stand rooted and grounded
Thanking God for the blessing
Of being able to experience
Many of life's different misfortunes.
For I know that all things
Work together for the good.

And am glad to have received
A bad day than no day at all.
So you see our maker,
No matter what he has in store
He's always on the inside working
For something bigger and better
To genesis on the outside.

Our Lord, yes our Lord.
He has provided.
Provided days and nights
Of opportune enhancement.
Of what? Simply that of the obvious.

Altered Conscience

But only to you.
Only to shape and mold
Into something of magnificent composure.
For edification of the spirit of the body,
As well as the revitalization of truth.

Our God has made this possible for me and you.
He has provided a way to remove the mist
From our dreams and awaken hope.
He has provided!

Reginald L. Russell

REJUVENATED SOUL

As I come back to the intersection
That has twice been repeated.
I take a look at my life's misfortunes
And contemplate on them.
Feeling that thought will do me more
Than a hand full of good.

But it hasn't.
My initial thoughts were to be all
That the Lord would allow me to be
But it is of the obvious
That those feelings
Have been subtracted
From my train of thought.

So here I am
Standing in between the two roads
Trying to make up my mind,
Wanting to heal my body
and settle my soul.

Altered Conscience

Comforter what do I do?
It has been many years now
That my soul has been dead
To the cautions of this old world.
Struggling not against
The unrighteousness of this world.
But in every aspect
And in every capability

I have yielded to this world of fragility.
Digging myself deeper and deeper into a hole
Which I would soon come to find to be
A burial place for my soul.
Prepared by me!

Comforter what do I do?
I am a soul of lost stability.
So as I come back to the intersection
That has twice been repeated.
I look back at the misfortunes of this 'ol life
And remember the burial place
Prepared by myself
And as I approach this grave
I place Something there,
It's a garment of shame
Which I am proud to say
I no longer have to wear.
My rejuvenated soul.

Reginald L. Russell

ANEW

From a distilled heart
Filled with venom
I take time to reflect
On my trials and tribulations.
Remembering them as if
They were a wound on my side.
Coming out of a world
Where the reality of my dreams
Are faint and bleak.

Trying to fight my way
Out of this horrific encounter.
I often ask myself
Is this life worth living
If I am to live it
In heartache and pain?

Through my blood travels
A lifetime of iniquities.
In my knowing of this
I attempt to live
And be someone
That I know not of.

Altered Conscience

How am I to live like this?
But as I act out one
Of the greatest characters
I am compelled to say
That of this life,
This way I want no more.
Life is meant to be lived free.
I want to live free of hurt,
Free of sickness,
And free of pain.

As I act one
Of the greatest characters
I am compelled to say
That of this new life
It will not be the same.
For the emotions
And feelings that flow,
They will go
To the overflowing River
That leads to me no more.

Reginald L. Russell

?QUESTIONS?

The solutions to life's equations I do not have.
Just questions,
Questions that add on
To life's mystical evolutions
And create a mirage of hope for the hopeless.

Questions that allow people
To think, dream, and wonder
About the realization
Of life's gospel truth.
Pure questions.
Some of rhetorical stability,
And some of very High intellect.
Pure questions.

It may wander through the brains of some,
Why it is that questions are manifested repetitiously.
Intriguing some

But causing most to run,
Run from their prophetic and definite arrival.
Not even willing to penetrate its nucleus
And figure its structure.
Scared or are we nonchalantly turned off
By its revelation?
Just a question.

Altered Conscience

This, this is my style, my way.
Reggie's way.
Reggie's way of releasing
The anguish and anxiety
That living life brings.
Slight hesitation along
With brief animation
Always willing first
To let the realness in,
Shutting his eyes to the false.
But always opening them to the grim.
Why?

Let me be the first to say
That Reggie has never been a saint
On any heaven-made day.
I'm just as you
Trapped in a maze
Of sacred sorrows
With this "S" on my chest
Standing not for super,
But suppressed.

Reginald L. Russell

But by whom?
I don't know,
But it won't be easily forgotten
For my heart,
That it has consumed
Allowing my mind no room
For any digestion of this.

But my soul is in constant battle,
Trying to reconcile all incidents
And situations that occur.
Yeah this is Reggie's style,
Reggie's way.
Particular to no other.
When will Reggie be complete?
Questions, pure questions.

Altered Conscience

HAYSTACK

I stretch forth my hand
Reaching toward the haystack
Wanting to pull away from a success
Concurrent with no other.
Can you define my independence and stability?

As my day rolls away
I look toward the night
Which shows me a providence
Of a day unknown.
Eliminating all deceit and disillusion
Orchestrated in time before.

As I stretch
I recognize many of Life's inconsistencies,
Allowing me not the opportunity
To gather myself and prepare
For tomorrow's frantic revelations.
I often wonder if I should be given
My piece of the haystack,
But thinking to myself
I remember the words
Of a familiar authority saying
"Son if it's not worth working for
It's not worth having."

Reginald L. Russell

So I stretch forth my hand
Reaching toward the haystack
Wanting to pull away from a success
Concurrent with no other.
Can you define my independence and stability?
Living my life not for the prestige of today
But for the joy of tomorrow.
Progress, progression;
Success, succession.
Can these institute
A feeling of worth
And Allow me to feel
As if my stretch is meaningful?

I stretch forth my hand,
Reaching toward the haystack
Wanting to pull away from a success
Concurrent with no other!
I dream of a dream,
I feel of a feeling,
I progress in progression,
I succeed in succession.
My haystack.

Altered Conscience

REGGIE'S PRAYER

Although, Reggie is a man
Of many self-dependencies.
He realizes his weaknesses.
Yet throughout his life of secret gossips,
He being the topic, hid himself!
Running from his prophetic purpose,
Trying to become something
That he's really not.
How familiar?

I speak to the Lord my God
For there is no one else
Who understands me.
Realizing the error of my ways.
Coming to my maker
Most humble and submissive.
Taking notice to the fact that
I am no greater today than yesterday.

Lord I come to you asking
Not of material possessions.
But in search of love
Which only you can give.
So Lord please, restoreth me
The joy of my salvation.
Amen.

Reginald L. Russell

REGGIE'S PRAYER 2

When I say that I'm hurting,
Who really listens when I express that?
I just can't seem to press my way any further,
Who really cares after I've stopped dreaming my dream?
And the reality of life has crushed my hope,
Then what's next?

When you say
That you understand, do you really?
When you reply, "I can relate,"
Can you really?
When my soul has decided
To prolong its long-suffering,
Do you understand that which I fathom?

My soul and flesh do tarry.
Sometimes I wonder
The significance of this life,
Anxiously awaiting my departure.
The world expects me to qualify myself,
But is this my sole purpose?
If not, then why do I indulge
In such things,
Even unto the Love that I hope
To one day have as my wife.

Altered Conscience

When I go to her
And tell her that I love her
And she replies not back to me,
Is there any significance
In why my heart aches at her silence?
Should I be concerned?
I've loved her for a long time
And possibly have been dreaming
For a long time too.

Could it be that
My mind, body, and soul
Are flooded with that
Which is unattainable?
I have worries in this life,
And all that which I desire to do
Is eliminate my pain and my strife.

It has become painful to love.
My heart seeks a joy
That which no man can give!
And my mind,
My mind seeks its resting place.

Reginald L. Russell

I shout unto my only strength
"Give unto him who asks of thee
A new heart and a new mind."
For that which exists in me is of no use.

Provide unto him who cries out, a healing.
A crucifixion from the old
And a resurrection to the new.
Amen.

Altered Conscience

TELL ME
PART 1

Up the street
About two blocks from here,
There's a man standing on the corner with a beer
Looking as if he has been disillusioned
About why he's there.
Tell me do you know why?

Down the street
About a couple of blocks from here
There's a fair young lady
Standing on the corner
With fine attire
And an un-meaningful stare.
Standing there looking
For someone to take her higher,
As if she's been disillusioned
About why she's there?
Tell me do you know why?

In the middle of the city
Where things are sidity
Resides a family
Whose problems and nightmares
Are far past birth,
Looking for a way
To break this repetitious state.

Reginald L. Russell

And within that home
There stands a man
With his right hand rolled to a fist
And a hand full of hair in his left
About to strike a devastating blow.
Tell me do you know why?

In the room nearby
There's a child who holds his cry
Allowing his situation
To get not the best of him.
Plotting and preparing,
Waiting For the opportune time to avenge.
Tell me do you know why?

In a house on the hills,
Where we look at the moon and stars for thrills.
I look at the many different dramas
That go on under the light of the sun and moon,
And as I look I ask myself what I see
As it appears it's nothing new to me.
And in all the problems existing in life
The main ingredients are pain and strife,
Tell me, do you know why?

Altered Conscience

TELL ME
PART 2

Trapped in the state of denial
Residing in the city of gullibility
Near the ocean of frantic notions.
Neither knowing how or why.
Somebody, anybody tell me why?
Why this person of manipulation
Is existing in my life?

Somebody, anybody tell me why?
Why someone can take
That little white Rock,
Put it in a glass pipe or fry it
And put it in a needle and abuse it
Until their heads are in the sky?

Somebody, anybody tell me why?
Somebody, anybody tell me how?
How a mother can use
And abuse her kids?
Not really realizing
What she's done.
Scaring her kid's for life
As she's standing on that corner
Looking for pain and strife

Reginald L. Russell

As if that two minutes gig
Can fill that vacant love needed
From on high.
Somebody, anybody tell me why?

Somebody, anybody tell me why?
Why a brother particular to no other
Can end his own life?
Is life that hard?
After all, what difference does it create?

'Cause before long
It won't matter
If you have a hit song,
Or a house on the hills
That gather thrills,
Or an account
With a steady amount.
It just won't matter.

Are these the most important of life?
Somebody, anybody tell me why?
Why a mother and father
Live their marriage
In a regretful way?
Not realizing what
They're really leading astray.
Discombobulation.
Somebody, anybody tell me?

Altered Conscience

Somebody, anybody tell me how?
How we can turn away
From this erroneous state
And move into a haven
And relax by an ocean
That allows us to concentrate
On life's heavenly destination.
Somebody, anybody tell me?

Reginald L. Russell

COURSE

Many don't understand my flow.
But I know the direction it goes
Once I passed through the forest
Of blue and red,
I saw hope it was dead.
Dreams they are asleep
And faith Is bleak.
Love is awaiting on high,
In precious hands of dove.
All awhile hate lurking
From side to side
With his head swollen,
Full of pride.

But no one else knows.
They walk around
As if there are no darts in their backs
Nor faces that have contorted, awakening curiosity.
Living life as if they were some kind of inevitable force,
Incapable of being conquered.

I once passed the forest of blue and red,
And that I also saw hope and it was dead.
But one thing that I failed to mention
Was the river of suspension
And that with its appearance,
The most uncertain sense of dissension
Accompanied.

Altered Conscience

As I passed,
I saw Someone there.
A man with long hair
And a dreadful stare.
He invited me to a drink
And from it I became befuddled.
So it was a safe assumption that
On that day I drank with disaster.
I feel my life flowing faster and faster.
With direction undetected.
Contradiction? But what is this force?

As I walk throughout life
With my destiny, unacquainted.
I hear a voice of familiar authority.
Asking how it is that I made it this far
And upon whose help have I depended.
I reply on yours and no one else's.
He instructs me to give up all attention
And that he'd take care of the rest.
Through this life of subjective disillusionment
And particular distraction
I yield, I yield, I yield!

Reginald L. Russell

DREAMS

Dreams flying my way,
I'm conscious of the next day.
I'm trying to live right,
Suffering ain't in my blood
So I hustle day and night.
Tell me if I'm wrong!
I hum a slow tune
While my mind sings a fast song.
Appreciating life for all that it offers:
Death, sickness, pain,
And the quick adaptation to change.

I'm fascinated
And empowered by the mystery
Of what tomorrow brings to my life.
Hoping maybe the next day
Will bring no pain and strife.
Detached from fantasy,
Lacking prosperity
And drunk from reality.
These have manifested as my plight!

Altered Conscience

Have you ever wondered
To wander far, far away?
To elude the sting
Of Life's inconsistencies,
I bridge my heart
With a sufficient amount of fear,
Yielding to neither this nor that;
Steadfast, only to react off fact.

I've hoped from life that
Whatever created wrong be made right,
As well as the departure of every good thing
Pave a way for something even better to replace.

I struggle between right and wrong,
Thus constituting my instability.
I breathe the distraught emotion
Unbalanced from normality.
I figure the strength of my life
Is the realization of my weaknesses.
Balanced and proportioned
Only by what my inner self sanctions,
Particular in whom I deal;
This is my life.
Focused on a dream
Set to secure my tribe.
I strive for the mountains
But In the hills I hide.

Reginald L. Russell

TROUBLE

Trouble in my soul, I'm tired;
I want to go home!
I've drifted far, far away.
The realization of my life's misfortunes
Has caused me to go astray.

It's too late to dream,
So I guess I'll scurry on to hope.
The truth of my life I hide
As I place it under my cloak!

You see my face daily,
The expression of a vibrant life.
But on the inside I battle
Between wrong and right.
Why has God chosen this road for me?
My free agency to find joy and happiness
Has been nulled,
Leaving me discomforted
By my single choice,
Unable to plea.

God has spoken,
I've heard his voice.
A certain thought lingers in my mind
Pushing me to make a choice.

Altered Conscience

Guide my feet Lord
Cause I've lost my way.
Place your tongue
In my mouth, father.
I'm not too sure what to say.
Shackle my hands from destruction
While you construct in me a new living creature
For everyone to see?
Amen

Reginald L. Russell

RAIN DOWN

Rain down on me Lord!
Allow me to reign
On my life's transgressions!
That crown you once wanted
To place on my heart,
I stand here waiting for procession.
I agree father that
I have been disobedient to your will,
And throughout my inconsistencies
You loved me still.
I want to bridge the gap
Between you and I
With a serene love
Set far from a dream.

I've imagined myself with additives.
Purposed for destruction.
I've ran from your love.
Headed in hate's direction.
I've been wounded
By the snares of this 'ol world
And by these have incorporated
My true wealth in society.

Altered Conscience

In their eyes
I amount to nothing,
You see me as a king!
Lord help me to correct what can be;
And that which cannot,
Allow those hurt to see a different me!
My soul has longed for the day
That my heart would have courage
Enough to declare a change,
Father I yield to rearrange.

I've done everything imaginable
To bring peace to myself;
None of It worked.
It ended only in hurt!
I'm now eager, father
To do your work!
I stand before thee on this day
Searching for a healing,
'Cause I've surely been hurt!

Reginald L. Russell

DREAMS AND WONDERS

Dreams, I have dreams so many
Yet so few to come true.
Oh Lord what shall I do?

I dream of a vibrant future,
I dream of a world
Where racism, bigotry,
Sexual immorality,
And drug addictions
Are not the common denominators.
I dream of coming home
To a family facing no problems.
I dream of looking into a mirror
And seeing an image with no blemish.
I dream.

Wonder, I wonder far beyond
An average imagination
And in my own create a labyrinth of joy.
Making an elaborate effort
To concentrate on the good things
That life brings.
I have wonders so many
Yet not knowing why I do.
Oh Lord what shall I do?

Altered Conscience

Although I wonder
And although I dream
What good does it bring
Besides provide an outlet
For me to get away?

In all my dreaming and wondering,
Could it be that I am trying to hide my face
From the gruesome light of tomorrow
Or trying to block the hideous path of yesterday?

My life I have tried to live
To how it is painted.
I have dreams so many
Yet so few to come true
And I have wonders so many
Yet not knowing why.
Oh Lord hear my cry.
I have dreams and wonders.

Reginald L. Russell

DOTH FOLLOW

My heart doth follow
The joy of tomorrow
Seeking it like a bee seeks its nectar.
My brain seeks the e=mc² equation of life.
My soul it doth wonder
Through the thick-coated factions of this life.
My flesh it doth yearn for pleasure,
Only looking out for itself.

Can someone tell me why?
Why the pain of yesteryear
Overshadows into the new sunny days
Of tomorrow
Causing it to rain?
Why my thoughts are clouded
With that of the undesirable?

All these feelings,
Ideas, questions, and thoughts
Are they necessary?
While always in my seeming
They are never taken into consideration.
Can someone tell me why my heart,
My brain, my soul,
And flesh doth wonder?
For I know not. I know not.

Altered Conscience

DO YOU KNOW ME?

I'm posted on signs
Of broad lines,
Expressing myself
In the best way of capability.
And just for you to see,
Do you know me?

I feel just as you're wondering
What to do in my time of distress.
I bleed the same color of blood
And eat and drink just as you.
Do you know me?

Am I yet familiar to you?
Have you ever experienced a time
When life was written on small lines,
Not big enough for you to see?
Has your heart crushed in an instance
And created a point of no existence
Leaving you with the feeling
Of unhappiness?
Do you know me?

Yet in all of this despair I still seem to care
If you…know…me.

Reginald L. Russell

CAUGHT

I guess my #'s up,
All my dreams and desires gone;
What the F*&^!
I planned on gettin' my s#$& right,
Who would have known?
All I needed was some time.

Now I'm looking down
The barrel of a chrome 9,
Concerned about my life?
Why should I be?

I should have been more concerned
When I stomped that N$##@
Out in the street.
But I was only lookin' out
For my N$##@,
I would have never thought
He'd come back squeezin' a trigga!

I tried to find some true motivation in life,
But all I found was sorrow.
How could this be?
I'm a child of God.
He promised my life would be bearable
With his help.

Altered Conscience

I wouldn't have to worry
About my health or wealth.
So I'm blessed.
Life is changing and so am I.
"Which road do I take?"
As I look to the sky,
My heart is troubled
With iniquities that I cannot bear.
I'm beginning to wonder
If anyone cares.

Someone one day asked
"What it is I wanted out of life."
I took a deep breath and recited
All of my wants;
There were a few from too many,
The person sighed
As if I'd said something wrong,
Shaking his head as he strolled along.

The truth about my life is that
I always wanted to live right.
The love of God filled me up,
But the devil ran away with my cup.
So now I'm dry, every day
I'm getting high.

Reginald L. Russell

I remember momma telling me
"Son that's the wrong road to take,"
And so I walked away
Conscious of a decision to make.
The things that I've done wrong,
Lord I'm sorry
Please let me live on.

I know it's not that easy,
Your son is drowning in iniquity.
Everybody says that I'm no good,
But they don't understand
That I'm just trying to make it
Out the hood,
And I'm willing to do what…

Yes of course father
I know that on you
I'm supposed to rely
But you're taking too long
And my life is short;
I've gotta ride.

Altered Conscience

I refresh and reflect,
But da pain is just too strong.
The s#&% I did yesterday
Just won't leave me alone.
My dreams are dead
And my hope is not too strong.
I'm struggling to finish
But my struggle won't last long.

I guess my #'s up,
All my dreams and desires gone;
What the f*&%!
I planned on getting my s#*% right,
Who would have known?
All I needed was some time.

Now I'm looking down
The barrel of a chrome 9.
Concerned about my life?
Why should I be?

I should have been more concerned
When I stomped that N*&&$
Out in the street.
But I was only lookin' out
For my N*&&$,
I would have never thought
He'd come back squeezin' a trigga!

Reginald L. Russell

NEVER THOUGHT

I never thought for a moment in my life
There'd be a time I put the Lord
To the back of my mind.

Always thought
That my success was through me.
Never took the time
To thank the Lord for blessing me.
But that was a time
when my eyes were blind.
I didn't really realize,
But now I know
'Cause he gave me something to sing
And shout for. Yes he did.

All of my sin and grief I bear,
It's the result of my neglect
Towards my lord's precious grace.
My initial thought was
To run and hide my face
But through my running,
My false sayings,
My life of perversion,
My lie of sin,
The Lord has slowed me down.
Embracing me with his agape love.

Altered Conscience

How do I get back
To the road of divine truth
And serve my Lord with my all.
I never, never, never thought.

Reginald L. Russell

MY DREAM

A distorted imagination transformed
To cohere with that of reality.
A lifetime, a journey; what follows?
A dream? My dream? "The dream"?

From a field full of bland emotions
A questful revolution begins.
Wait a minute!
No one blew the whistle!
I got ahead.

Wrong?
Hey don't clog my dream!
Feel my desire,
Give evidence to my zeal,
And my corruption,
Provide for it a place of shelter.
My dream, feel my dream.

Help me push past life's cataract.
And rescue, rescue my dream
Out of the hands of a fate doomed
With a kiss from despair.
My dream, feel my dream.

Altered Conscience

Explore my rugged horizon
Surfaced by pieces and fragments
Of broken hearts surrounded
By an unequal opportunity.
My dream.

Allow my soul to be free,
Allow my heart to listen
Before my mind utters
Insignificant words.
My dream, feel my dream.

Reginald L. Russell

THE PERFECT CHANGE!

Last night I had a dream
That everything I wore gleamed
And wasn't nothing funny
About my money,
And you could see my stack
From way far back
And that was a fact!

Everything I touched glittered
And everything I envisioned came to life.
Wasn't no more pain,
Wasn't No more strife
And folks was proud
To be living life.

Ain't that something?
'Ol Tracy from down the way
Ain't doing no more frontin'
She's shoutin' hella hallelujahs,
Talkin' bout how the Lord
Done brought her out.
And all I can say is, amen.

Altered Conscience

And you know what else?
Ms Jackson from 21st street
Finally "hit" that damn lotto.
She was hoopin' and hollerin'
About how the Lord
Done answered her prayers.
She won 20 million!
She told momma that
She'd been praying for
A financial increase
Since her second child, Kiesha,

Kiesha's twenty.
I reckon God blessed her
With a million
For every year on her knees.
Ain't that something?
All I could say was, Amen!

Reginald L. Russell

BLACK WORLD

Black world, black world
A place where fathoms are always
A common and dominant ingredient
In our mixture.
A place whereby
Every Swallowing of a crumb
Makes one more hungry
For the prestigious life
This country offers.

Black world, black world
A place where just by the pulling of a trigger
Has ended the life of a thousand young N*&^#
And I do mean N*&^# Niggas
Who at any opportune time
Had the chance to graduate
To a status of a brother.
And in the declaration of his manhood
It would be different from all the others.
Yeah only in a black world.

Altered Conscience

Only in a black world
Would a brother leave a sister
For another of a different color.
Not that that's wrong.
But that doesn't match
The lyrics of our song.
Though love is blind
We need to take the time
To lift our sisters up.
Lift them to an assurance of our love.

To erase this misconception
Of her being not even equivalent
To a common tramp.
When in all actualities
She's supported and comforted us
 From day one until the day new.

Black world, black world,
Only in a black world
Are we so quick
To reveal that life brings
And guarantees nothing
But a hard way to go.

Reginald L. Russell

Black world.
Only in a black world!
I mean we're here.
We walk, talk, dream and aspire
Just as everyone else.
It's hard for me to see
The drastic difference
Between us all.

So is there really a need
For our own world?
Or is cohesiveness not important?
Black world, only in a black world.

Altered Conscience

IF NEVER

If never before I've seen this
I've surely seen it now.
With all the problems
Existing in my life,
You came and surely
You calmed them down.

Since the first time
My eyes gave heed to your beauty,
I knew you were the one.

The one to take this drama
Out of my life
And make room
For the ever-shining sun.

My yoke of equality,
Yeah that's you.
Someone that I can just
By talking receive joy.
Believe me,
I look at your face of vibrance
And I receive happiness.

Reginald L. Russell

Never before in my life
Have I ever felt this way.
Please label me not as a fool.
This has got to be love,
Because to me
There's no greater feeling in existence.

If never before I've seen this,
I've surely seen it now.
With all the problems
Existing in my life
You came and Surely
You calmed them down.
If never before!

Altered Conscience

ONE FACE

Bitter emotions engraved in my soul.
Living life for the curiosity of tomorrow.
Engaging in activities
That lead to sleek sensations.

Revealing the obstinacies of my life,
Leaving them for all to see.
Rebelling against the ordinary life,
And in all my knowledge,
All my knowing
I try and create something new.

The imagery of this great world
Has brought me nothing of its testament.
Yet you wonder why I rage.
It's plain enough for all to see
That life's not what it's meant to be.

Different promises made to me
Look at my hand rolled to a fist.
How many kept? Can you see?

Reginald L. Russell

The truth fabricated from day one.
Leaving you hopeless,
Feeling that this life
And this way can't be undone.
Knowing the requirements
And expectations of this world,
I regret to say to yield to these
I won't be the one!

Despite my proclamation.
They want me to lose it
And find a new one.
Thinking to myself
With a frown on my mind
I reply and say well
That would make two faces.
I only need one.

Altered Conscience

STRIVE

Our forefathers have come and gone.
Brought from a land of happiness,
A land of only our essence.
Only to be placed
Into a labyrinth of hell. America!

The home of the brave
And land of the free.
Yet my eyes are deprived
To see just how free,
And my heart has been deprived to know
Or maybe they've been deprived to show
The bravery.

Please label me not as a racist
But label me as a realist.
For I only tell it
And show it to you
Just how the portrait
Has been painted.

Reginald L. Russell

Envision kings and queens
Once rulers of a vibrant and rich soil.
Struck down from their throne
Having their garments of respect and dignity
Stripped from their breasts,
And made to be housemaids and field hands
And objects of sexual gratification. A thrash!

That was our gracious welcome
To this foreign place. Robbed.
We were robbed of our heritage,
And made to speak their language
And learn their ways.
How to make feast
Of their throwaways.
Yet in all of this we strived.
Oh hearken not your heart
Brother and sister
There is seemed to be one
Who cares intensively
Of our well-being.
His name is Abraham Lincoln.

Altered Conscience

Yet in his concern
His objective was not to free us
But only to leave us as a people
Holding on to a promise.
No, no! In no way do I defame
The character of the great Lincoln

But in my claiming of no defamation
I add nothing to it.
They've fed us these color-coated,
Truth-binding promises
And we've opened our mouth to them
Waiting for the opportune time to bite down.

But through all this despair we strive.
We strive for a better tomorrow.
We strive for the promise.
We strive in one nation under God.
A nation that promises liberty
And justice for all.
We strive, we strive
In continuous search for promise.
We strive.

Reginald L. Russell

BLIND EYES

Blind eyes, blind eyes.
With blind eyes I see you.
With a blind heart I love.
With a held tongue I talk to you
Only releasing the graceful words
From up above.

It's been so long
Since we've talked it out.
We argue and we fight
Not knowing what about.
Are we actually that different
Or Are you so full of hatred
That you can't even find
The slightest room
In your heart to love me?

Our forefathers have stepped in and out
Of boundaries violating each other
Causing decades of conflicts.
But there's a new day, a new decade,
And a new generation of kindred.

Let us forgive and forget
The violations contributed
And see and love each other
As though we were blind. Blind eyes.

Altered Conscience

OH, HOW REAL

Sitting at the river of ironic notions.
Holding myself from the hypnotic waves
That pass by, intriguing me to jump in
And become one of hypocritical residency.

Lying down on my back
Looking up to the sky
Drooling at the manifestations
Made clear to me by God himself.
Oh how real is this?

Gawking at the birth of my newborn son.
Contemplating with a smile on my face.
All the while thinking that this is me.
The fruit of my offspring. My clone.
Oh, how real is this?

These are the fruitful things that life brings.
The happiness of being able to control oneself
And feel the freedom of spirituality.
All these a gift.
How real is this?

Reginald L. Russell

The ability of being able to point out
God's magnificent masterpiece
Which is everything that surrounds me
Oh how real is this?

The realization of God's gift to us all.
This that we partake of with God,
Will never fall.
Oh how real is this?

Altered Conscience

MY DAY

When my day comes,
I want to be ready
For that freedom train.

When my day comes,
The day when my Lord calls
My name from that mighty roll,
I want to take nothing with me,
But leave everything behind.

I will talk with David,
Elijah, Moses, Peter, and Paul.
But first, I want to talk to Christ,
And ask him his thoughts and feelings
Toward his brothers and sisters.

Yeah, after I cross that river called Jordan,
I will glorify the Lord with all my heart and soul.
And all things of me will be anew.

Reginald L. Russell

MOMMA, WHY MY HEART?

Momma when I wept last night
I wept over a love.
Over a love that proceeded from my heart
But never entered into another.
I thought repetitiously how I possibly
Could allow myself placement
Into this circumstance.

I never imagined
Even unto the most extreme of imaginations
That I would fall a victim of a sealed heart,
That the first of loves would be the one
To discourage me from initiating
Any emotional involvement ever again.

I have murdered the possibility
To capacitate a love for another.
And have given birth
To a venomous heart.

Momma when I wept last night,
I wept over a hate.
Over a hate that proceeded from my heart
With a high intent to hurt.

Altered Conscience

REALISM

In the mind of a man
Distraught to think
Or so he thought,
A revelation begins.
Reality has shown herself!
She has arrived
And with her accompanies
A new season

With no seeds sown and nothing reaped.
A season ready for the impact of an intellectual
Who was at one time blind.
Who was at one time consumed
With a misconception of life.
Who was at one time boggled
With living through life's pain and strife.
But reality has shown herself!
She has arrived
And with her accompanies
A new season.

In his new season
His began had become his beginning
And his beginning had just begun
Leaving no ties to any unrighteous ones.
He's detached and manifested in a different light,
A light so bright
That it illuminates his path on the crossroads.

Reginald L. Russell

HOW I LOST MY WILL

I watch my life blend
Into the sunless days and nights,
Torn into pieces I separate the fantasy of my life
For something much more real and unsatisfying.

I desire to tune my life
Toward making myself happy
And dissolving despair.
No one ever desires to separate their souls
From its reason for existence.

How does one's life become entangled
And suppressed from comfort and joy?
The engine of my heart is running low on fuel;
The ability to run is vastly approaching absolute.
It's time to find out what I'm really made of!
It is time to make certain of my reality
While filtering the rubble.

Tear away from disenfranchisement and uncertainty,
Breed a new love for existence
And get a head start on a new dawn,
Pull life's chords as if it were a brand-new guitar!
Tune in to your song and dance away,
No more time in life to worry about misfortune,
This life is lived by those who choose;

Altered Conscience

It's choosing time,
Don't wait in line.
Find that desire and passion
That once fueled your life,
Believe in the courage
That stands you
On your two feet every day.

Have faith in God
To believe that all things through Christ
Have made you capable
Of actually living your life
And not letting your life
Live through you!

Reginald L. Russell

ALL STARS MUST FALL
#94 RUSSELL

Lord, they say you're not real
But I know that you are!
Their words pierce my side,
not my heart.

Our relationship proves enough to me.
The lies that I hear
Explain the dis-concern of your love.
Who wouldn't want something
So precious from up above.

My heart grows strong,
But my mind grows weary.
It's hard out here fighting this fight!
I love you, Lord, yet struggle amongst
What is wrong and what is right.

Please, Lord, handle my plight!
Sow your heart in my mind
So that I have no choice
But to do your will.
Without your help, father,
I know that I won't survive,
I would soon die.

Altered Conscience

Having built a life surrounded of lies.
Father, please hear my voice.
I feel stuck in the world
Afraid to make my own choice.
I am bound by your blood
And fear your everlasting anointing.

My dream is to one day walk in your glory!
I pray without praying a blessing
For my life to be molded by thee.
Father, I commend thee
To resurrect your love within me!

I shall now submit my ear and my voice
To the echo of Calvary's purpose.
I now render unto you fully
My life as a complete and total sacrifice.
Lord, deliver me always
From evil temptation,
Allow my feet to be quick
In response to your will.
Hold me high
So that mine enemies might believe
In your goodness!
In the name of Christ, I pray.
Amen!

THANK YOU

Thank you for reading and enjoying this story. The purpose of releasing these archived writings was to hopefully inspire and/or encourage a young person trapped in a very subjective lifestyle. There is hope at the end of the tunnel when we focus and redirect our frustrations in life; the goal is to get in alignment with God's will and not our own. Things were going very wrong for me in my life at a particular point in time; it was not until I began to circle back around to where I left God that I began to experience life in a more impactful manner. Please share this book with young adults everywhere in hopes that it will provide a lamp unto their pathway! God is love and remember to keep it Christ centered!

Lastly, I want to honor my wife, Mrs. Brandi Russell.
She has blessed me with 5 beautiful children
And continues to support me on my journey.
The Lord blessed me with an "Angel",
She is my teammate, lover, and friend.
She is the best,
Here's looking at you
"My Love"!

www.ingramcontent.com/pod-product-compliance
Lightning Source LLC
Chambersburg PA
CBHW071620040426
42452CB00009B/1411